I0421918

Reading People

Learn how to analyze people to identify unique personalities. Gain perspective, and use the best approach that applies in today's society to deal with any behavior pattern

KEITH COLEMAN

© Copyright 2019 by Keith Coleman - All rights reserved.

This content is provided with the sole purpose of providing relevant information on a specific topic for which every reasonable effort has been made to ensure that it is both accurate and reasonable. Nevertheless, by purchasing this content you consent to the fact that the author, as well as the publisher, are in no way experts on the topics contained herein, regardless of any claims as such that may be made within. As such, any suggestions or recommendations that are made within are done so purely for entertainment value. It is recommended that you always consult a professional prior to undertaking any of the advice or techniques discussed within.

This is a legally binding declaration that is considered both valid and fair by both the Committee of Publishers Association and the American Bar Association and should be considered as legally binding within the United States.

The reproduction, transmission, and duplication of any of the content found herein, including any specific or extended information will be done as an illegal act regardless of the end form the information ultimately takes. This includes copied versions of the work both physical, digital and audio unless express consent of the Publisher is provided beforehand. Any additional rights reserved.

Furthermore, the information that can be found within the pages described forthwith shall be considered both accurate and truthful when it comes to the recounting of facts. As such, any use, correct or incorrect, of the provided information will render the Publisher free of responsibility as to the actions taken outside of their direct purview. Regardless, there are zero scenarios where the original author or the Publisher can be deemed liable in any fashion for any damages or hardships that may result from any of the information discussed herein.

Additionally, the information in the following pages is intended only for informational purposes and should thus be thought of as universal.

As befitting its nature, it is presented without assurance regarding its prolonged validity or interim quality. Trademarks that are mentioned are done without written consent and can in no way be considered an endorsement from the trademark holder.

How to make a killer **First Impression** without embarrassing yourself, even if you're socially awkward and can hardly start a conversation

To sign up for my free author newsletter and get your free copy of the first impressions guidebook *Key Impact*, visit

bit.ly/kckeyimpact

Table of Contents

INTRODUCTION

Congratulations on taking the first step to explore your innate socializing skills!

This book will help you to understand how to use your intuition to start reading people from their verbal and non-verbal cues and how to put all the information together in a crystallized form in order to utilize it effectively.

Reading people is a skill that we all have inside of us. Non-verbal communication is something that we are continually experiencing in ourselves and in other people. It is something that you can tap into and find in yourself, rather than trying to develop it as a new skill.

Reading people is something that is deeply innate in humans, and anyone who tells you otherwise is not being truthful. You can find the way in yourself, and you will be able to decrease your stress and the stress of others if you tap into this instinctual resource.

The following chapters will also discuss ways for you to know yourself better so that you can read other people. You will learn how mindfulness can become the seed to grow the tree of your identity, and when you start the journey towards self-realization, you will start to experience greater ease in your relationships, work, spiritual, and emotional life.

Please enjoy.

Chapter 1

UNDERSTANDING BEHAVIOR

To read people, we must evaluate the information that is accessible to us. In some situations, it is possible to have a conversation with a person that will clear things up. However, that conversation is not always possible. So, the behavior is what we are left with to evaluate. This includes body language, actions, and other observable aspects of a person.

There is a whole school of psychology devoted to the study of behavior. In fact, this school states that behavior is the most dependable source of information with which we can use to read others.

B.F. Skinner was a hugely important American psychologist who came up with the concept of behaviorism. Behaviorism was his school of psychology, and it has since grown to be one of the most researched and acknowledged sects of psychology. Behaviorism is focused on being able to cultivate quantifiable data and analyze it to observe behavior. Once data is collected on behavior, then the behavior can be analyzed and changed.

Think of a cat that is being trained to ring a bell for a treat. The cat is shown how to physically lifts their paw over and over again to hit a button that produces a sound. When the cat is shown how to do this and then given a treat, this is creating approximations of the desired behavior. In this instance, the desired behavior is for the cat to hit the bell and produce a sound. The reward is the treat, given when the desired behavior is produced. This creates an atmosphere that supports the behavior with a reward making the cat more likely to begin and continue this behavior on its own. There are huge applications to this, in parenting, schooling, a nod in the science of behavior in general.

In the above example, the treat acted as a reward for the desired behavior. This is known as positive reinforcement. In the context of behaviorism, we don't think about things as positive and negative in a "good and bad" sense, but rather, in an additive or subtractive sense. When you add something to the situation, whether it is a punishment or a reward, that is a positive act. Positive just means that you are adding something instead of taking something away. A positive reinforce or a positive punishment is when you add something on either end, that is, adding something unpleasurable or adding something pleasurable. Rewards are also known as reinforcing because it reinforces good behavior. A negative reward or negative reinforce would be when you take away something that is difficult or unpleasurable when the desired behavior is produced.

So, in the scenario with the cat, you could apply any or all of these strategies. You could apply a positive reinforce, which would be a treat for the cat. You could apply a negative reinforcer. This would be something that you have affecting the cat and then when the cat pushes the button (the desired behavior), then you take the bad stimuli away. Maybe this would be something like spraying the cat with a bottle of water until the behavior is produced. This is just an example to illustrate the options of negative and positive and punishment and reinforcements. If you were looking to decrease a certain behavior in the cat, like sitting on the bed, and then you spray the cat with water each time the cat produces that behavior, you are applying a positive punishment. If you take away the cat's favorite toy when they sit on the bed, you are applying a negative punishment. The probable option for actually modifying the cat's behavior is positive reinforcement. Positive reinforcement has been studied over and over and has always been shown to be the most successful way of changing behavior. The other methods of applying punishment and reward have repeatedly shown to increase shame and can increase poor self-esteem.

This is all to say that behaviorism is such an important tool in reading people because Skinner has laid out the basic groundwork for a way to understand how behavior works. It is pretty simple, in this scheme. A person reenacts behavior that is rewarded. When something is rewarding a certain behavior, people do that behavior again and again. There are also other forces at work on the punishment side. When the punishment for performing certain behaviors will stop those behaviors, but not always, there are conflicting forces to be sorted out when applying the principle of behaviorism.

Behavior is only part of the story. It is not the whole story, but it is the most observable thing about a person that we can tell. Some behaviors match up with what they feel inside, and others don't. Being able to read this congruence (consistency or matching) or incongruence (inconsistency or not matching) can be a big tool. For example, some people need to grieve by having a quiet place to share their lives with themselves and only be with their memories than their own body at that moment. Other people have different grieving traditions and needs. Some people need to celebrate the life of the deceased person, and that is how their grief is expressed, through the celebration of a person's life. Often, we have different relationships with different emotions. Some are skilled at expressing their sadness and aren't good at expressing their anger. Some people are good at expressing their happiness but have difficulty expressing their anxiety. By observing this in yourself, you can observe it in others. The relationship that a person has with any given emotion will define their behavioral response to an emotion. A good example of this is the widely varied presentation of behaviors in children. A kid who is "acting out" may just be trying to express a certain emotion, whether it is anger, or a less obvious emotion, like grief or fear.

When emotions are repressed, they will build up and leak out in maladaptive ways, rather than being expressed regularly. Maladaptive behavior is when a behavior is working toward an end goal, but with the wrong means. Addiction is one major way that maladaptive behavior is used to address problems.

An addict creates a relationship with a substance because the substance does something for them. It is no secret that a substance, like a drug, will bring people to a different state of consciousness. Sometimes, it is an upper; sometimes it's a downer. Some people like to use drugs to get them more excited and energized, and others like to take drugs to bring them down. Drugs have very complicated and subjective effects, so this does not mean that there is a binary separation between two types of drugs, but it is an easy way to simplify things.

An addict finds a way to treat a need that they have with a drug. Maybe it is that they feel bored and tired, and they want to find something that will let them be excited and energized. Let's say that they start taking Adderall when they are tired. They start doing this when they have a busy workday, and then later, when they have a less busy workday, they are slightly more likely to use the drug. They used it for a need before, why not do it again? It will start to slow down the effects of the drug, and the person will start off experiencing things differently. Soon, they feel that they need it. They start to adjust their emotions, behaviors, and thoughts to be centered around whatever can let them get by, and soon, it is not helping them but rather, hurting them.

The "acting out" problem which was mentioned earlier also serves as an example of maladaptive behavior. When a kid is acting out, they have a need that is not being addressed. That might be to get along with other people and impress peers, or it might be to protect his or herself, or it might be a need to feel strong. Whatever it is, the need is addressed somehow by acting out. Let's say for this example that the behavior is getting in fights with other children at school. Maybe it is a badly placed need to interact with others, and the child has not found a way to interact with others in a healthy way. Maybe the kid likes physical activity, but the sports that he has access to are not interesting. There could be all kinds of reason for the acting out. Maybe his family life is very unstable and anxiety-producing to the kid, and so fighting is their way to make sure that they have some control in the world. Whatever the need may be, it is being addressed through fighting; it is just not being addressed in the right way. This is the key; you must look for the counterintuitive reason for a behavior. You must look beyond the obvious. Instead of concluding that this child just likes to be aggressive, or is unskilled at getting along with others, you should realize that the child has learned a maladaptive way to cope.

Yet another example of maladaptive behavior is when people cheat in relationships. When a person has agreed to be in a relationship where there is intimate exclusivity, and then they go against their word and get involved with another person, they are being cruel and unkind, and it is important to acknowledge that. However, there is probably also some sort of need that is not being met in the relationship. Sometimes it is just the sexual need, but this is not always the case. Often with this person, it is a need for attention, for love, or for intimacy that is not being met in the relationship. It could be something as simple as boundaries not being kept that the person has never spoken up about to their partner. This can create deep problems in the relationships, and even though a person didn't want to, they find themselves violating the boundaries themselves when they are in a situation where it is possible.

All of these scenarios demonstrate how maladaptive behavior can come from the expression of need. It is not what it always appears. When you are dealing with some sort of behavior that seems to cause trouble, ask yourself if you can identify what the need is that someone is trying to address. They are just trying to address their needs in the wrong way.

Reading people happens in a split-second; it happens when you see a person walking in the door. Your ability to read people will be affected by how much you are able to observe from a person. If you see them walking into a room, but they then leave, you will get much less information than if you get to have a whole conversation with them.

When you do get the chance to have a conversation with a person, make sure you are asking questions and being a good listener. Being a good listener means fully concentrating on what they are saying. You almost have to take it as a gestalt with some people, because you can't hear each individual word, but you get the overall picture. Sometimes this is necessary. You should look at them in the eye and observe their eye contact. This will tell you about their confidence and directness. You should see how they are standing, how they hold themselves and how they speak to you. Then, just trust your instincts, and keep yourself from getting distracted. Some good tools to use for conversation are reflecting, or saying what the person said back to them, or probing, asking about something that they left out. You need to operate on a micro and macro level to read people, and you will need to know the specifics, but also be able to just describe the person in general to "the vibe." Often a person will have energy; trust your reading of the energy, and know that you can go with this gut instinct.

Here are some specific strategies to understand behavior:

1. Try to put yourself in their shoes.
    Try to understand what the person is going through and try to imagine yourself as the person that they are. This is empathy, and it is important in reading people.

2. Show an interest in others.
    When you are interested in others and ask questions about them, you are demonstrating that you

want to know more about them. Showing interest in a person doesn't mean that you interrogate them. Just be friendly! If you are interested in them, then act like it. People will be much more open if you are open with them.

3. Ask open-ended questions.

Open-ended questions allow for answers that will tell you a whole lot more about the person than just a yes-or-no question. Open-ended questions are more like, "What was that experience like?", or "How was that for you?" It doesn't put restrictions on what you are expecting as an answer.

Chapter 2

ANALYZING BEHAVIORAL PATTERNS

The cat example, which we discussed earlier, is pretty easy because there are some clear-cut behaviors that we want from our pets and there are some that we don't. Pets are easy to see the effect of behavioral principles, because they're driven ultimately for food and self-preservation, along with bonding.

In humans, however, it is more difficult to parse why a person will act the way they do. They might be driven by unconscious drives, or they might be hiding their behavior from the world. It is always impossible to know what a person is doing behind the scenes.

First of all, you can establish a baseline. This will not be possible if you don't have any context or history with a person. However, if you do, you should determine what that person's "normal" is. Most of us have a "baseline", our default personality or way of being. The baseline is how we are naturally. Someone's baseline might be that they are anxious. This is not them reacting to a certain stimulus or situation; it is just how they are. We probably know a person who goes naturally to anger when problems occur. This is their baseline. Some people have a tendency toward depression, and that becomes their baseline.

What does it take to change a person's behavior? Well, here you can just remind the person that they have committed to being somewhere at a certain time, and that they should respect the boundaries of their work item and be there for when it starts. This is if you are responsible for the person's behavior.

If you are not responsible for working with a person, or otherwise have no reason to try to change the behavior, then all patterns must be accepted. This is hard for some people. Some people want everything to work out and be good for them, and they don't know who to accept the world around them.

Acceptance is key here. Accepting behaviors means you don't judge whatever a person is doing. You can know that their behavior is self-destructive or bad for others, but this doesn't mean that you can't accept their behavior. Acceptance does not mean condoning. What it does mean is that you realize the extent to which you can affect someone else's behavior, and it is looking at the patterns, which are observable and drawing conclusions from there.

Patterns are observable only in one way to us. It is important not to make assumptions about a person based on their observable behavior patterns. Patterns are merely the data that you have about a person. As an example, a person might drink a cup of coffee every morning. Let talk about how much we can surmise just from this one single behavior pattern. One is the aspect of addiction. We can know that this person, judging from this one behavioral trait, has the capacity to be addicted to something. Pretty much all of us do. You cannot for example, judge that this person is an addict and can't keep themselves from doing this. But a cup of coffee in the morning is an addiction.

Patterns can give you insight into the motivations of a person. If Sarah usually ends up hanging out with Mark rather than Jessica, this could be from multiple factors. It could be that Mark has a love attraction for her, and that her drive to be in a romantic relationship is more important to her right now than her drive for friendships.

People can be read because people's lives are a story. People have individualistic things that make them unique and themselves. Each person has a life story with many chapters, and each person contains multitudes. It is not a question of if you are able to read people, because people will show themselves to you. It is the question of if you will be able to read them and use that knowledge for your own good.

When you are trying to read another person, try to focus all of your attention on them, but still while observing them in a neutral way. Check out their posture. Are they standing up straight? Are they crouched or leaning to one side? This can tell you about the physical state of their body. Older people often lean into their posture and will be a bit more hunched over. This is a sign of age. Sitting up straight is a signal that a person is relatively healthy and young.

When people walk, they tend to lead with a certain part of the body. Some people lead with their heads, some lead with their feet, some lead with the chest. This can give you great insight into the person's drives and how they conduct themselves. A person who leads with the chest may be proud and strong, and they like their physical appearance. If a man has shrugged shoulders that hang down and leads more with the waist, this gives you the idea that they are carefree and laid back. If a woman leads with her hips, it means that she is feeling confident. There are all kinds of ways that body language can give you insight into a person's personality.

One of them is how touchy or physically affectionate a person is. Some people like to being hugged, and they live to connect physically on a basic level in everyday life and conversation. Other people are not so comfortable with physical contact and prefer to eschew hugs for handshakes and a nod of the head. Neither of these is correct, as there is no correct approach to this. You just have to be cognizant of the boundaries that exist, i.e., not hugging a person who clearly doesn't want the physical contact.

The next main point to consider when you are reading people is the affect. What do we mean by

affect? The affect is the way that the face is expressing thoughts and feelings. A normal affect is considered one that has a wide range of expression, as an
example, smiling when one is happy and having facial expressions that match what one is saying and doing. The affect is a big clue to how someone is feeling. People with mental illness can have flat affects.
This means their affect does not change much when
they say different things, and they're not able to express feelings with their faces. This comes with various conditions. However, much less severe cases of
restricted affect can come simply from being shy or
anxious or sad. A person may restrict their affect
when they have social anxiety, to give an example. A
person's thoughts can be wildly swinging all over the
place, and their face is displaying a neutral, calm reaction. This can be a protective mechanism for some
people, for when you hide your emotions, you and
other people don't have to deal with the messy reality of where your emotions are. Some people display
all of their feelings with their face. When speed reading people, you just have to determine how much a

person's affect is actually representing their feelings. Then, you can engage.

Eye contact is a huge part of this. How much eye contact is the person making? Is it sustained and intimate? Is it broken up? Sometimes, people can be aggressive with eye contact, and it can actually be a way for people to act out their dominance in a situation.

Eye contact is a proximal thing that can connect and divide people. The term male gaze was coined to describe the interaction in eye contact or gaze alone. The male gaze is what it is due to the power of the eye. It is something that we often forget, but eye contact is a powerful tool when you make eye contact with someone, you are making a connection. This connection might frighten some people, and people who are shy or have problems with self-esteem will often avoid eye contact to a high degree. This eye contact is causing a primal level of connection that they do not trust because they don't trust themselves, and they don't have confidence. A person with confidence can make eye contact with anyone they encounter and engage with them. People might be intimidating, but you can always engage with someone in good faith and have confidence in yourself to represent yourself and your ideas effectively.

The only way to start reading people is by practicing. You can give yourself practice by intentionally putting yourself in a situation where you will be around other people and trying to observe them. Observe their tiny movements, try to see how they hold themselves by looking into their eyes. Do not try and linger, just try to make the interaction as normal as possible, with observing as much as you can about the person.

When you get home, write about it. Try to recreate whatever you saw and observed in the person and try to get every little detail known onto the paper. Try to describe what you saw in that person's emotional state, their affect, their smile or lack thereof, their body language, what words they used, and everything else.

Here are some practical strategies to analyze behavioral patterns:

1. Analyze a person's drives.

    If you ask Freud, the drives are always unconscious and often related to psychosexual development. He believed that there were ways that people developed, and if they didn't get to a certain stage, they would be stuck in that stage, which would affect their unconscious drives. You don't have to think about it in this context, however. You might determine that a person's drives are for money, or friends, or romance. Just try to see what the person wants, rather than what they represent themselves to want.

2. Analyze where a person is in their life.

    This is a big part of analyzing behavioral patterns. Older people have different motives and different needs. You must consider a person's life journey when you try to account for their behavior.

3. Consider the baseline.

You can't know anything until you know the person's baseline. This is how they usually act. It is their default orientation to the world. A person's baseline is from where you must start when you are trying to analyze their behavior.

Chapter 3

NONVERBAL
COMMUNICATION

Nonverbal communication is a huge part of your life, whether you realize it or not. Each time you talk to a person, there are tons of messages that are being conveyed through the slightest body movements. When you experience this, you are just talking to the person, and you are listening to what the person is saying, and you are using your mind to connect with them. However, your visual, smell, hearing, and other senses perceive tons of information that is being processed automatically.

Consider this saying: "Language is a blunt force tool". This is essentially saying that language does a pretty good job of what it purports to do, but is messy and destroys a lot in the time it takes to do the job.

This might seem a little abstract at first, but once you consider the complexity and depth in the human experience, you can start to understand why it makes sense. What is language supposed to do? It is supposed to convey thoughts, ideas, concepts, and stories to other people accurately. It gives us a way to interact and puts us all on one level of communication so that we can make simple messages to each other and get by. However, language is also responsible for transmitting the most important and deep and abstract concepts. What it comes down to is the complexity of our everyday experience. How could you actually describe the flow when you're replaying basketball and making every shot? How could you really describe that in words to someone and have them actually know what you were experiencing? What about when you eat a piece of chocolate? Get broken up with? These are things that cannot be described in words, and yet we try to describe them. Sometimes it is done in ordinary conversation; sometimes it is done in art or literature.

Language is what mutes and bottlenecks our experience into what we are able to convey to other people. Language is so limited in its ability to share our experience with others truly, and it is that limitedness that makes it so that body language is so important.

You are often experiencing both at them at the same time; you are experiencing someone's language simultaneously with their body language. Nonverbal communication is not all just body language, but a huge part of it is body language.

Body language is composed mostly of a few factors: affect, posture, and motion. Affect refers to a person's facial expression. If a person is smiling, you could say that they have a bright affect. A person's affect is not always congruent with what they're saying and experiencing. You might these this from someone who is talking nervously about something, and they begin to smile. This means that their expression does not fit whatever they are talking about and that there is incongruence in their affect. When a person has a congruent affect, their facial expressions will change and be malleable. A person who has a congruent and secure affect will be expressing whatever they're thinking about or talking about on their face.

Posture is the way that a person holds himself or herself. This is often derived from a person's way of being in the world or their general philosophy of the world. Our way of being in the world makes up our personality. Some people are oriented as warriors, others are oriented as perfectionists. The way that a person's personality is will dictate the way they hold themselves physically. In acting and improv, there is an exercise often done to help people act out their character's attitude. It involves "leading" with the body in a certain way. When an actor leads with a certain part of the body, it clues the audience into the character's personality and motivation. A proud person will lead with their chest, a sexually-driven character will lead with the hips. This type of thinking is all about symbolism and archetypes. When a person leads with their chest, they are leading with their heart. Get a little creative! Realize that this symbolism is important. What does the heart symbolize? It symbolizes pride, passion, love, and vitality.

What would the chest be doing on a person who did not feel confident? If a person is not confident, they will be not is leading with the chest, rather it will be collapsing. Think about a person who is not confident, and how their shoulders move forward, and their posture seems tired or broken. They are the ones without confidence because they are trying to protect their heart.

Posture and body language are not the only aspects of nonverbal communication. Nonverbal communication involves other forms of expression as well, including art. When we talk about art in this sense, we are talking about the capital "A" Art that includes sculpture, writing, acting, and all the creative arts. Even when language is involved, it is not verbal communication, it is writing. All of these fall under nonverbal communication. Learning to participate in artistic creation can help you to be a person who is more in touch with this part of communication.

Some people do not have the power of verbal communication. As an example, sometimes the power of verbal communication is lost when folks develop advanced dementia or other mental disorders including schizophrenia. Others could be people with learning or developmental disabilities like autism or Down syndrome. Can these people still communicate? Absolutely! Language is not necessary to communicate. Some ways that it might be easier to communicate with people who are nonverbal are touch, music, art, or hand symbols. People who are nonverbal tend to experience are in a deep way.

Some people have learning or developmental disabilities that prevent them from reading nonverbal cues. People with Autism Spectrum Disorder have a hard time deciphering the cues of behavior and non-verbal communication. ASD is a somewhat mysterious condition, and it is only diagnosed and marked by certain behavioral patterns and insufficient social ability. In order for kids with ASD to be able to function better, they have to be helped to have sensory integration. This means that they must learn to use their sensory inputs in concordance with their cognitive abilities to learn what a person is expressing. They will have to learn that when a person has their face all scrunched up, and they are yelping, that a person is angry. They have to learn about the body language of a sad person, and who to act around that person.

This is pretty much what we are doing in this book, except we are talking about it on higher-level. Rather than teaching kids how to learn the basic cues of nonverbal communication, we are trying to encourage you to learn to trust your intuition and analyze behavior patterns on a deeper level.

This means when you experience a behavior pattern, you can surmise what this means for you and what it means for other people around you. Instead of thinking about your feeling and worrying about it, you can either express it or act on it or do whatever wiles they need to do.

This is where the intuition comes in. you've got to trust what you are feeling about a person. If you see that a person walks into the room with a smile you've known before, and they act a certain way that you saw a person act, and you can know that they are trying to deceive you, this will make your life a little bit easier, as you can have that knowledge going in.

If you start to go to a new church, and at first you like it because of the community, but then you start to feel it is just not the right place for you, this is intuition. We can use intuition to the behavior patterns of other can know if they will be good partners, good friends, etc.

Here are some specific strategies for understanding non-verbal communication:

1. Try to use archetypes to develop an understanding.

   Is your friend playing the victim? Does your boss always want to be seen as a hero? Does someone want to be considered an artist, or a troubled soul? There are often archetypes which we can draw upon to develop an understanding of a person. Someone might be drawn to the healer role or the teacher role. You can use these archetypes to break down the defenses and see a person's inner drives.

2. Try to be receptive to nonverbal communication.

   Imagine you had to deliver a message without using words. Would you dance? Would you play charades and act out the message? Trying these things can help you to understand how people communicate nonverbally and this can help you to have a deeper understanding of this style of communication.

3. Try to analyze the tone of voice.

    The voice is very complex and messages that are delivered by the voice tend to have a lot of information that is not just in the actual words that a person is saying. The tone of the voice can tell you if a person is really saying what they want to say, or if they are not matching up with their true intent.

Chapter 4

THE SOCIAL MEDIA AGE

An increasing amount of attention and connection that is available to the average person has marked the social media age. Back in the late nineties, a person would create a website for themselves or for their business through traditional methods, and the technology was much less ubiquitous than it is now. A person who wanted a whole web page devoted to themselves was going to have to work to achieve that and hire people to create a website. Now, each person can have his or her own webpage, hosted on a social media site. This becomes their website, their journal, their business page.

This is a radical shift from the beginning days of the Internet when the website was scarce, and you had to find the stuff that you liked. Now, there are a few major corporations that run the social media sites, and they provide pages to everyone that wants one. These companies have worked to integrate their websites with mobile smartphones and computers so that the user can experience these websites from their mode and per a part of the action.

A few social media sites are the ones that everyone uses. So, there is pressure for you to participate in social media. Most people do it, so when a person doesn't participate in social media, it is considered strange or out of place. Social media has become the way that we share our world with others, and tell stories. There are many viral videos and pieces of content that are shared instantly thought-out the world, and this is the power of social media. It is a place where ideas can light a fire and spread through the world in a moment's notice.

However, what is the dark side of social media? It has created a world in which we think that we are judged by our social media personalities, rather than what we are actually doing in our lives and feeling in our hearts. It takes meaningfulness out of communication, and it places communication more based on technology than actually being present with someone.

When you are present with someone, you are able to look at their face and involve yourself in a constant feedback loop with them, and you perceive their body language, and you get a real sense of what the person is like and what they are conveying to you.

Text is much more limited. Text is how we communicate a lot these days, whether it is posted on social media or just text messages to friends. Text is not the same as being with a person. Digital text is even less powerful communication than a phone call because at least with a phone call you can hear the person's voice, which is a great expression. With text communication, however, you only get whatever a person is able to write down, and as we established before, language is a blunt force tool.

So, the social media age has made us more afraid of being ourselves. We want to put on a certain image to the world that says the message that we think we want to be perceived as. This could be that you are cool or smart or popular. Most people want to be portrayed as attractive and successful on social media. It is the age of FOMO, or fear of missing out, and that is reflected in our behavior. The fear of missing out is the feeling that people describe when they perceive that people are having fun somewhere because of their online posts. People see the posts and think that this person has the life that they want. They feel that they are not good enough to have the type of interesting experiences that these people have, and it makes us feel bad to be ourselves and raises all sorts of issues with anxiety and coping.

The phone begins to be a way of coping with anxiety for people, and they start to check it and participate in social media or whatever else to just reduce their anxiety. This can be an okay tool in some situations, but in others, it starts to take over from more healthy ways of coping.

When kids learn to use devices as coping mechanisms to escape from the world, they start to learn that that is a proper way to deal with anxiety. If something comes up that makes them feel uncomfortable, they can retreat to social media, where the connections will make them feel like they're supported.

It is important for kids to learn coping mechanisms other than this so that in life, they are not bogged down by always wanting to escape into their phones and looking at screens.

Sometimes a person has the habit of separating himself or herself from whatever situation they are in by using their phone in the company of others. This makes them disconnected, and instead of truly being with the people they are with; they start to never really get a connection, and they stay to themselves. This can disrupt relationships because this person is always wanting to set something up in the future or thinking about past events, and they never spend their time in the present. This is what social media does; it takes you away from the present. It is a way to escape, and American life has always been about escapism.

There is some main pathology that seems to come from our current social media landscape, and one of the main incidences seems to be anxiety. Anxiety is a natural feeling that humans encounter. It comes from the evolutionary need to protect us from the environment and form tether humans and animals. Back when people lived just before and during the hunter-gatherer phase, people had to protect themselves from the wild and unpredictable forces of nature. We don't have to live like that anymore, but these anxiety impulses are still within us. This has affected the human race since the dawn of the industrial age.

When the industrial age began, humans started to become disconnected from the things that they used to make, the foods they ate, and the things that they needed to survive. Before this happened, the creation of goods was uncentralized, and this led to a completely different landscape of how we got along in the world. This was before we were able to mass-produce items and it was before we were able to make things on the incredible scale that we are now. The industrial revolution completely transformed the lives of humans in the West. Rather than being responsible for making things and feeling in touch with the land, humans now were subjected to cruel working hours, and productivity took over as the main value of the land. Previous to this, people spent time with the goods that they had and the food that they ate. People were responsible for making things for themselves and master tools in the process. The mastering of physical tools lends itself to the mastery of metaphysical tools. This disconnection can be seen now.

This disconnection between what we eat, what we use, what we do, and who we are ha caused all kinds of problems in our society. We don't grow our own food; we buy it from the store. We have never met the animal that we eat every time we buy meat. The animals live far away, and the process of butchering them is not our problem. This goes the same for other products and foods. Those tomatoes you are eating had to be picked by someone; they had to be picked and grown and taken care of. We don't do that stuff anymore, and what this has led to is anxiety.

Anxiety is produced when we don't feel that we have power, and we feel that we don't know what to do. Anxiety is, to a certain extent, a natural phenomenon in humans and animals; it provides us with a safety mechanism that springs forth our fight or flight response in order to protect ourselves. In this way, anxiety is important and good. However, many people now have an imbalance in their anxiety, and they have little reason to be afraid.

However, they still feel anxious, and the level of threat that their body is telling their mind is there is really not there. This affects our interactions, our relationships, our ability to relax, and every other part of human everyday functioning. It makes us nervous, and there might be thought content that goes along with it. Worry and anxiety are closely related, but they are not the same thing. Worry is more about the thought content that comes along with anxiety. Anxiety is the physical feeling, and the worry is the thought content that you are focusing on.

What is the main thing that is missing? Real connection. This is what social media uproots. Real connections with the world are important for almost everyone in the world. While there are some parts of social media that actually do let us connect more to the world and to others, there are many aspects of it that leave us feeling disconnected and fail to ever increase our level of connection with the world.

However, it's not about the technology itself. It's about how we use technology. You can use a flower vase to display flowers or bash someone over the head. If someone is using Facebook to connect with relatives that live far anyway, and they are not able to visit much anymore, then that is great. In this case, social media has been able to foster a connection between families that were inconvenient or impossible before. This is great, and it is not the technology that made that happen, it was the person. However, if a person is obsessed with looking at pictures of their peers, while feeling insecure about themselves, and always checking in with their phones and never being in the present moment, then they are not using the technology well, and they will have to learn to change their behavior if they want to feel better.

Some people are able to use social media for their advantage, and others are not. Some people may find themselves wrapped up in what they read and see online, and they will start to question their own lives. They will start to feel that they are empty, or that their lives are boring, or not as interesting as other peoples'. This is because they are not getting enough real human connection in their lives. It is sad to see, and the paradoxical nature of this phenomenon is such that when a craven person is trying to portray themselves to look good on social media, those who can see through it broadcast these images. Instead of looking good or cool, they are broadcasting their insecurities to the world.

Which, actually, doesn't sound like a bad thing. Broadcasting your insecurities to the world is something that a confident person would do. That is something that a person who doesn't give a crap about what other people think of them. However, there is the problem of intention. When people are making posts, they are not aware of what is going on. They are just completing the cycles in their mind. They get a dopamine hit every time they post something or get likes a post. It has a built-in reward system, and social media websites are designed to draw people in and get others ever engaged with the site.

The smartphone has become a big problem with people on how to deal with problems of anxiety. The phone is something that we all carry around, in our pockets, in our hands, in our bras; we carry them everywhere, and no matter what we are doing, the phone must be nearby. There are some great technological advances that have been made because of this product, and there are incredible implications for the good that the smartphone can do in the world.

However, many people are not so good at moderating their behavior when it comes to cell phones and smartphones, and they get addicted. It becomes basically a little computer that we carry around, which is capable of playing TV shows, radio, all kinds of media, as well as performing countless tasks.

It can connect you to any page on the Internet. You can take a picture wherever you go.

There are so many functions that this contributes greatly to our addictions. Our addiction to the phone is always on the borderline between pathology and helpful; each person will have to learn where their lines are. A person who uses their phone too much might just have to learn to slow down a bit and be more mindful at the moment. Some people are not really able to have a good time with friends when they're hanging out, just because they are checking their phone all the time. It is a compulsive thing that they do, and it is to feel connected. This person should ask himself or herself, why can't I feel connected at this moment? Why can't I feel like I'm here with these people?

Our smartphone addictions must be moderated to the point of some rules. One good rule to have is that you never take your phone out during a conversation with another person. Some people like to treat the phone as if it is not in their pocket at all when they are out and about, and only use the phone when they need to use it for a specific reason. Some people will turn their phones off. Some people will just try to ignore it.

You should ask yourself some questions if you are feeling antsy and couldn't concentrate and feel like you need to be on your phone constantly. You should ask yourself, "Why can't I just be doing whatever I am doing right now, and not focusing on my social media sites?" It might be because whatever you are doing is not interesting. That's fine! You can find something else to do, something that you can be engaged in. There are times throughout the day when it is fine to check the phone. When you are on a lunch break or need to just decompress from the day, you can use the phone as a skilled coping mechanism by trying to distract yourself from stress or anxiety.

Here are some strategies to use in order to help yourself be more cognizant of the effect that social media has on you and others:

1. Pay attention to how much time you spend on social media each day.

   Are you able to sit quietly for ten minutes by yourself without reaching for your phone? If so, then that is great. If you are not able to do so, try working on your tolerance to being with yourself. If you are always distracted by checking your social media accounts, then you will have trouble making the connections that you really need to make in the world.

2. Observe how a person acts on social media versus in real life.

   If there are some inconsistency between how a person portrays themselves in life and on social media, then you know that they have some insecurities. This does not make them a bad egg; it just means that they are dealing with some anxiety in regard to the way that they are perceived by others. Try to understand why the person feels this way.

3. Look at the personality that they are describing with their social media presence.

   What is the person worried about? Maybe it is that they are concerned that people won't think they have enough friends. Maybe they are concerned that they won't appear active or busy enough.

Chapter 5

UNDERSTANDING PERSONALITY

There are many personality systems that have been redeveloped in the history of human study. Throughout time, people have engaged in self-reflexive exercises to explore what it means to be a human and why we are the way we are.

One of these folks who was studying what it meant to be a man was Carl Jung. Jung did a lot of writing and research on archetypes. Archetypes are relatable things that we all see in life. See, Jung thought since we all had common experiences -the sun, the moon, the dark of night and the light of day, and that this connects us with a collective unconscious. Humans have universal experiences, like birth and death, and love and heartbreak, and that these universal themes suggestive a psychic pre-ordained order in our minds. This is the idea that since we are all in human bodies experiencing the earth, there must be a commonality in our experience. These archetypes might manifest themselves in different ways in different cultures, but they are deeply held within us.

Since we are all connected to our physical experience and the earth in a very intimate way, there are forms of ways of living and personality that have come out into the consciousness as recognizable ways that people are the way that they are. The shadow is a symbol of the unconscious, and it is an analogy for a person's dark side, in the eyes of Jung. The shadow self-mirrors Freud's id and is the animal side to our consciousness. It is what makes us fully human, and it is the place that we go when we are feeling animalistic in any direction, i.e., satisfying a need to have sex, eat, or protect oneself.

Jung's work has been processed over and over again and has influenced many spheres of thinking, including popular psychology and scientific psychology. The Enneagram system is a system of personality that may have ties to Jung's work, as many of the principles that he looked at are found there. The Enneagram has its roots in the Sufi tradition, and it was refined over the years by various thinkers. The Enneagram of personality loosely aligns with Jung's idea of personality, and it presents nine personalities as ways that we can recognize people behaving in the world.

The Enneagram is not a magic scroll that will tell the future and tell you exactly how a person will act in any given situation. Rather, it is a way that you can think about personality and a way for you categorize people into behavioral patterns and tell why they are the way they are and why they do the things that they do. It is not something that is crystal clear in every case. A person who you see one day might act a certain way because they are feeling a certain way, but then the next day they will act completely different. This does not discredit the Enneagram, for the Enneagram is one the closest things to describe the indescribable. Like Jung's stereotypes, these personality types can be deeply tied to literature, movies, etc. and we tend to see them over and over and over in art and literature.

The Perfectionist

The first personality type in the Enneagram of personality is The Perfectionist. The Perfectionist is driven by a moral drive. They are good people, and this is because they grow up wanting to be good people. The Perfectionist will often have pathology relating to perfectionism. If a Perfectionist is driven in childhood always to be achieving and always trying to be the best, they can often grow up with habits that relate to perfectionism that will become problems later in life. The Perfectionist wants everything not only to be working in good condition, but they also want things to be moral. They see the world in good and bad, and they definitely want to be on the good side of things.

The Perfectionist will need to learn to calm down their perfectionist urges in order to reach self-realization. Self-realization is eating concept of a person being able to be fully themselves and reach the potential theta they have in several domains. These domains include but are not limited to leave, work, relationships, art, and whatever else a person needs to function. When a Perfectionist can realize that not everything needs to be perfect and that they can just reaccept what is going on around them, then they will be able to make more connections with other people and with themselves, and they will find that they have an easier time in life.

The Helper

The second personality in the Enneagram is The Helper. The Helper wants to help people out, and they want the world to be a better place. The Helper will often find a helping profession, where they are working to help others in their lives. They might have jobs like doctors, therapists, nurses, physical therapists, etc. These people have a deep drive to help and be helpful. They want to give and be generous with themselves, and they expect other people to do the same. The Helper often gets into codependent relationships, where they want to help another persona, and they need the other person to need them. This can become an unhealthy dynamic, as the Helper is always looking for their next person to help even though the person will likely never change.

The helper must transition from this pattern if they want to engage in the practice that will lead to self-realization. A helper must realize that others can be helped, and they fill this role very well, but they must also acknowledge that they themselves need help nod they must learn to help them and accept help from others. When the Helper does this, they will learn that the world is not a bad and scary place and that they can actually be in the world and be helped by others, and that this will provide them with a sense of contentment. This is all about balancing your key traits with the rest of your consciousness.

The Achiever

The third personality type in the Enneagram is the Achiever. The Achiever is a very optimistic and charismatic person. They like to go to the top of a mountain because they felt like it. Or, they might have seen someone else go part way up the mountain, and they want to prove that they can achieve something greater than someone else around them. Achieving provides a way for this person to find personal growth and feel good about them. This is a way to position a psychic without the perfectionism; however, the achiever will eventually realize that achieving is only one dimension of human life. Achieving is something that we do when we need to move society forward, and it is essential that we have achieved in the world. However, the Achiever will have to learn about other aspects of human life, including loving, resting, taking care of others, and reflection.

Once an Achiever can do this, they will learn that achievement is not needed for them to win the love of others, they can have love just the way they are. Acceptance is going to be a big task for the Achiever as they go on in life and try to make deep connections with other people.

The Romantic

The next personality described in the Enneagram is the Romantic. The Romantic is driven by a deep need to make life meaningful, and they do it well. The Romantic loves oceans, fires, parties, sunsets, storytelling, drinks, coffee shops, bookstores, and the like. They want to live in one beautiful moment forever. They want everything to be beautiful, and they enjoy the melancholy of life. They like to revel in the sadness that life is, and they think of the human condition as a beautiful thing. The would prefer being out on the road performing with a band than working in an office. They like to get lost in books and poetry, and they are usually good at conversation with others. The Romantic is oftentimes an artist, and they will often try to live as a musician, artist, actor, or radio host. They are people who are creative and spontaneous. One dark side of the Romantic is that they are prone to depression. This is because they feel so much in the world, and they are escapists because the world overwhelms them. They may not be good at modulating their emptiness nod getting out of a certain mood state. They might feel that the world is too sad and dangerous for them, and this will often keep them in a depression.

To find self-realization, a Romantic will have to learn that not every moment in every day is beautiful. This will be where they need to find acceptance: not every day is beautiful, not every moment is a good moment. There are dry, humdrum moments that take up the better part of each day, and they will need to learn to cope with that. The Romantic will often temper their earlier instincts for chaos and rebellion and find peace. They do this through acknowledging that the world is not always beautiful, but it is nothing they can do about it.

The Investigator

The next personality type on the Enneagram is the Investigator. The Investigator is driven by a need to perceive the world. They may be web writers or journalists or scientists. They like to organize themselves in the world's sponge, somebody who is always receiving information from the world. They believe that by observing and investigating, they will find truth and meaning. They are driven by the need to perceive. The need to perceive is something that we all have within us, but the Investigator is obsessed with it. They might suffer from a lack of personality in the self because they're always focused on others and other systems and bodies to be convened with, than to investigate themselves.

In order to achieve self-realization, the investigator will need to learn how to turn that investigating light upon themselves and have space for self-reflection. The investigator could be aligned with many different worldviews, but this doesn't change their core need to balance their urges. This will take the Investigator to have some sort of life-altering experience where they feel humbled. Only then will the light be able to shine on the closet in their mind and really learn what is up with them and how they can live in the world and thrive.

The Loyalist

The next category of personality in the Enneagram is the Loyalist. The Loyalist wants to mother more in the world than friends. They don't like the physical intimacy of intimate relationships at first, and they are not so convened with family bonds. What they want are friends to surround them at all times and for them to have a full social circle with many different types of friends. The Loyalist will often have a group, or they might just have a one really good friend that they have found a symbiotic relationship with. They will find a person that they are able to accompany in the world and be loyal to, and the person who they are with will find ways to be a person that the person can be loyal to. The Loyalist really dislikes conflict, and they will want to avoid conflict at all costs. The Loyalist tends to get into a codependent relationship. Often times the Helper and the Loyalist will get into a codependent relationship where the Helper wants to help the Loyalist change, but the loyalist is not interested in changing, rather in prolonging the relationship. They will find themselves giving little of what the other wants at different times, and they will find that they get locked into relationships that are unhealthy and are really bad for them.

What the Loyalist needs to develop to reach self-realization is a sense of self and identity. They're so focused on themselves in the context of others, although the Loyalist will need to learn how to say what they want, and learn to be themselves around other people. Often times a loyalist will feel like the world has cheated them, that they were a good person and friend at that they are not given in the same opportunity back to prove that they are the best. They will feel downtrodden and disappointed in the world, and they will need to take this feeling and learn to modulate it. The Loyalist often feels that the world has some crazy order to it that they can't figure out. The Loyalist will need to learn that it is not the case; actually, the world is similarly indeterminable to all people.

The Optimist

The Optimist is the social butterfly. This is a personality type from the Enneagram that loves to be with other people and loves to lift other people up. They are able to see the good in every situation, and they have fantastical dreams about what could be in the future. The Optimist will be able to imagine realities that are not accessible to the everyday thinker, and they will be driven by the need to fix, to achieve, and to bring people together. The optimist may be less of an achiever, but hey have achievements in certain areas. The optimist loves to light up a room and make people laugh, and they want to see everyone around them grow to their full potential. The optimist loves meeting new people, and they love being around children. They think that life should be carefree and easy. They want everything to be a good time, and they want everyone to be partying all the time.

In order to reach self-realization, the optimist will have to become aware of that the world is a somewhat pessimistic place, and they will have to get more in touch with their feelings of sadness and fear. This happens slowly unless some kind of dramatic event ever happens to cause an ego death in the person.

The protector

The next personality in the Enneagram system is the Protector. The Protector learned early on that this is a way they can control their environment. They are good at helping other people out, but not in the same way as the Helper. They like to use strength to defeat their enemies and accomplish their goals. They are often really good at sports, and they tend to be people who emphasize the physical form more than others. They see the physical form as a metaphor for the mind, and where the mind goes, the body will follow. They see themselves as having a role in the universe to tend and to take care of others in an emotional sense, like watching out over a flock.

The Protector will need to realize a few things in order to reach their potential as a human being. They will need to learn that they, like everyone else, have weaknesses, even physical ones, and they will learn to live with these deficiencies by learning to depend on other people. This will be hard for the Protector, as they really dislike exposing themselves to others, and they hate being vulnerable. The Protector is a person who will need to learn to embrace the inner child, and rather than telling them that they need to fight to survive, they need to tell the inner child that it okay to cry, it is okay to be weak, it is okay to depend on others.

The Peacemaker

The final personality type that is presented by the Enneagram of personality is the Peacemaker. The Peacemaker is interested in harmony, and they like to be connected with other people, they like to see them thrive in the community. The Peacemaker is driven by a moral compass, but not in the same way as the Perfectionist. Where the Perfectionism wants everything to be perfect, the Peacemaker desires everything to be good because then everyone will experience less suffering and pain. One of them, pain, is never going to leave our lives. There will be aspects of pain, whether it is physical or emotional, throughout our lives. It is not something that we can escape. Suffering, however, is something that happens when he tries to deal with pain and can't really deal with it all the way.

In order to make peace with the world, the Peacemaker must actually go the other way and learn how to be more of a fighter. This is the mistake that this personality type often faces: they don't realize that to enact the change that they would like to see in the world, they have to go out and do it. They like to keep themselves out of battles. They need to be more like the Protector if they want to establish higher-level orders of consciousness. The Peacemaker knows when they are doing this. They must be able to learn how to stand up for themselves as well as others and to be assertive and fight the good fight.

The way that these personality types are situated in the Enneagram has significance, as well. There are triads and wings in the Enneagram system. These can be studied more if you are interested in the subject. The personality types presented here and other systems of personality basically give u a way to look at people and analyze their behavior. They can show us the way how people act in certain stations. They tell us about the innate drives of a person rather than just the venerable characteristics.

You must be careful in trying to apply the knowledge of personality types to your everyday life, and know that people might be tricky and may not be so easily figured out. On one day of the week, a person may be acting like a certain personality, and on another day, they might be in a big mood that differs from the other days. Depending on whoever they want to be at the moment, something different is to be expected. However, there are certain ways that we orient ourselves in the world, and these contribute to our behavior. The personality types can tell you how to observe these and what to look for. There are many other systems of personality, which can open your perspective even more.

Personality is something that is not set in stone, but it does tend to be a way that a person functions in the world for most of the time. People can shift, and a person may have to actually make the shift from fitting in with one personality to an entire different personality type in their lifetime. It is uncommon, but it does happen. There are ways that you can derive some meaning from the personality types listed in the Enneagram, and they can be a good way for you to read people.

By being able to identify a perfectionist, for instance, you can know why a person does what they do. When you realize that they might fit in well with the perfectionist personality type, then you can start to know that they want everything to be good and moral, and that is their highest motivation in life. Then you can adjust your expectations accordingly.

A big part of what the Enneagram allows for is for you to adjust your expectations of a person. Many people think about everyone as having the same characteristics as them. Some people may have similar patterns and characteristics as you, but many do not. Expectations allow for you to be able to know what a person will be able to handle, what a person can do in certain situations, and how much you can depend on them.

There are different thresholds that we all have in various areas. One of them is the discomfort threshold. Many people have high discomfort thresholds, and they're able to withstand certain types of pain better and longer than others. Some people have high emotional pain tolerances and low physical pain tolerances. Other people will have the opposite experience: physical pain will be easy for them to endure, but the emotional pain of vulnerability will be difficult.

So, using the Enneagram, you can make sure you are not expecting a Perfectionist to try and do some messy task with you and be okay with it, and you know not to ask a Protector to be vulnerable went there are other people around. You start to notice these patterns in people, and you start to notice their fears and desires and what makes them light up. The Enneagram can clue you in to why a person might be afraid of one situation and happy in another.

Let's talk about the applicability of the Enneagram for everyday life. Here are some practical strategies to help you use this personality system to read people and analyze them:

1. Start trying to categorize those around you.

   There are plenty of spaces which we can use for practice in this regard. When you are at work, try considering the different personality types in order to read people who you are around. The office assistant? Strikes me as an Optimist. That person in payroll who doesn't have a problem speaking up to protect others? Might be a Protector. Keep a list of the nine types accessible so that you can "diagnose" the folks who you can observe.

2. Don't use your knowledge as an excuse for poor behavior.

   When you learn about different personality types, and then you start to label those around you, be careful not to excuse their behavior when it is unacceptable. You might think, "That's just the way Sam is; he's a late person." While at a certain level, this might be true, it is important not to dwell on this label and let Sam get away with everything. Each person should be held accountable for their actions. This works on yourself, too. How often have you heard yourself think, "I'm not that type of guy (or girl)"? Well, have you ever considered that you could be that type of guy or girl if you try?

3. Be careful of projection.

Undoubtedly, you will identify with one of these personality types as you read through them. You might start to identify others who are just like you. This is great, and it shows that you are starting to be able to think analytically about behavior and personality. However, you must be careful not to project your own characteristics onto other people. Sometimes people with depression will wrongly assume that other people around them who are like them are depressed as well.

Another example: people might assume that others in their age group have the same ideological or political ideas. This is not always the case.

4. Take advantage of the differences in people around you.

   You'll find that there are plenty of friends, colleagues, and family who are much different from you. Take advantage of these differences as opportunities for growth and ease, rather than being afraid of differences. If you are a Perfectionist, and your friend is a Romantic, maybe ask them for advice when it comes to problems where you have to derive meaning in difficult situations. They should come to you when they have problems with motivation or directness.

Chapter 6

UNDERSTANDING BIAS

Human life does not exist in a vacuum. It's all about context. It's all about knowing the when, where, how, and why people are the way they are. Cultural upbringing and our family of origin shape us all. The culture that we grow up in has a great effect on our values, our career trajectory and other realms of our development.

In the USA for example, we tend to be pretty focused on certain values. Inarguably, one of these is making money. The entire structure the government is set up to be for the people, but much of it has been corrupted by the purposes of making money. Capitalism is what we strive to live under, but it is a certain type of capitalism, one that forces us to go to college, choose a job, and live a predetermined path. The reason for this is productivity.

Think about a life where productivity isn't the goal. What would you do? Maybe you would spend more time on art or writing or just observing what is around you. You might spend time on meditation, or just being with nature. Perhaps families would have more time to take care of each other and live happily.

However, we live in a culture that wants productivity above all else. Productivity is king; it provides money to the big guys. People are stuck working in jobs that aren't really leading anywhere, and we are just getting by. The forces that we jive under demands us to go to the work all the time and introduce huge stress and anxiety on our lives. If we are meant to be productive, where is the place in society for the weak, the young, the old, and the disabled? Where do they have a spare tube and live? This is a big part of the problem with our urgent society. People like the old, the young, and the weak are cast aside and not really paid attention to.

We tend to like youth and beauty in the US. When a person is not super young anymore, they become less interesting. The values that are often in older people are like wisdom. When a person has reached this age, they tend to learn about the world and start to be able to apply the knowledge they have to their every day and more abstract experience. Youth and beauty are seen as morally good while being a mess or being old are seen as reprehensible.

We have very strict structures around how people would dress in their country. The rules for dressing well haven't changed much in the last hundred years, and when a person is not dressed in the standard of what we perceive to be normal, we find them to be weird and unattractive. Attractive people are actually considered more intelligent even though they are not.

Studies have shown that we ascribe traits to certain people who we find attractive. This could be a movie star or someone walking down the street. Either way, we start to view the person as slightly different for being attractive. Part of this is our animal makeup; evolutionarily, men wanted to find women who would be good mates for raising children, and they looked for youth and body type in their search. Women were attracted to mates who could protect them and who had a social status that would enable them to have a good life. This is a structure of evolutionary psychology that still has remnants in our psyche today. It has since then been co-opted by advertising and corporations, and our need to be attractive overtakes us often. When we see an attractive person, we assume that they are more efficient and smarter than someone who may not be as attractive. This is just one example of how we grow up in a certain culture and start to think in the way of the culture.

We have a male-dominated culture, one that celebrates the accomplishment of men and emphasizes male traits. This can affect women and men in several ways. Sometimes it will include an internalized misogyny and will turn into a stewing heap of resentment. Other women recognize it and work against it. Their struggle to cope with the forces of oppression will shape the way that they live their lives. Men will also be affected by this society; bemused men are expected to act a certain way. They are expected to be Stoic and tough and never show weakness. To share emotions is to be labeled unmanly. They might find that they need to take special time to learn how to share and express their emotions.

These are all examples of the ways that society faces shape that we are. Peel will have all different types of personalities, no matter their gender or race. But the societal forces that they face will affect the way that their personality is addressed. There are multiple layers that contribute to reading people.

When you are attempting to read people, you need to take all of this into account. This means that you should not go from Nebraska and travel to a small island country in the Pacific and expect people to have the same value system as you do. This means recognizing where you came from as a way that you perceive the world and trying to understand that all value systems are objective and that people act how they were taught to act. It might take some time to achieve being non-judgmental, so try and put yourself in their shoes.

This will require that you use a great deal of empathy, and you will try to learn about a person through the way that they see the world, not the way that you see the world.

There are many different religions, faith systems, attitudes, cultural traditions, and many other differences that distinguish different humans on this planet. However, there are many common connections as well, and there are ways to understand other people's experiences.

One way to do this is to try food from other cultures. We grow up eating certain kinds of foods, and we usually get used to eating whatever our family ate. This is a great connection to the world that carries a sense of history and community to the family. This is all great, but it can also be fun to travel somewhere and try to eat the food that they eat on a daily basis. You will start to experience the layout of the culture a little bit more. There may be restaurants in your town that you never have tired. Try them, and see how it feels to put yourself out of place every once in a while.

Bias is not something that you should beat yourself up over. In fact, it is a way that you can know yourself more deeply and understand how you are interacting with the world. It can be a painful process to come to terms with your own bias, but ultimately it is something that you will need to face to become self-realized. Bias is just a part of the way that we fit into the world.

You also shouldn't confuse your own traditions and values for bias. In our super-woke culture, it is often hip to ignore the old-time things that our families have done or try to eschew tradition. Traditions are not what hold the bad, regressive views does. Traditions need to be upheld, the bad views or olden days can be dropped off without dropping off our culture. Many realize the mistakes of past generations, and they judge them fairly for it. However, we must remember to establish ways that we have cultural continuity and ways that we can come together as a community.

These are all examples of the cultural context that you must consider. Perhaps, you are trying to gain insight into someone who is not from the USA at all. Then, you will have to try to put yourself into their shoes. Maybe they are from a culture which highly values independence and individuality. Maybe they are from a culture which puts more importance on community and family. Whatever their cultural context is, you must use this if you want to gain any insight into who they are as a person.

Here are some strategies to help you remain conscious of yours and others biases:

1. Consider your family life.

    Remember, we didn't all grow up with you. Everyone had a unique experience growing up, and we all made different connections with ourselves and others. Some people had deep, intimate connections with their parents. Some people don't talk to them anymore. Some of us grow up with accepting parents, and some had to make sure never to make a wrong move. Consider others family life and the possibilities that may lie therein.

2. Ask yourself where your default is.

Ask yourself some key questions about what you value and what you think is important. These might include, "Where did I grow up?" "How did where I grew up affect how I see the world?" "Have I experienced other cultures, and do I have an understanding of the different values that exist in them?"

3. Evaluate your strengths and weaknesses.

You might be great at baseball. Not all of us are! Take an inventory of your special skills and where you are lacking, in your personal life, and in your work life. Make sure to recognize an equal amount of strengths and weaknesses, and don't use this as an opportunity to beat yourself up.

Chapter 7

KNOWING YOURSELF

Reading people involves keeping knowledge of how we see the world and how we move in the world in order to be able to observe others. This is why knowing yourself is so important. It takes a lot of intuition to understand how other people see you in the world, and this can cue you into their behavior.

One way to start this is to look at the Enneagram of personality and see what lines up most with you. This can tell you about what drives you in your personality that you might not even realize. When you are trying to find out what type of personality you are, you are engaging in a self-reflexive behavior that will help you to be a better person. If it will help you to know yourself and your intuition will be increased as a part of this.

Another way to know oneself is to participate in the art or to watch or listen to art. A movie can tell us the story of a world. It is a way by which we understand the world. Each time that you talk, you are telling a story, whether it is in the words, or in the way that you speak the words. This can help to see yourself of the weaknesses and strengths that you have.

When you are reading a great novel, you become immersed in that book, and you get to share a little bit of the writers' world in your imagination. The writer and reader create a continuum, wherein the writer's consciousness is being followed directly by another person. They say that literature is the art that most people can actually escape their world and get into another person's consciousness.

You start to learn the characters, and you start to predict what they are about to do. Characters in the story can be compared to people you know in real life, and the book can give you ideas about your own behavior and change the world in your actions. As you go out through the story, you are experiencing a ride that is the most joyous way of expressing ourselves. This is art.

Art is a mysterious way that we participate in. Art has the power to incite wars and peace. It is a way that you can deeply disturb people and you can keep them happy and calm. Art (we are talking here about the art with a big A, as to mean every category of art, from dance to film to sculpture) is a way that we are in the world that lets us start a feedback loop with the world, and it becomes a source of communication with the world and with others. This is a way that we can find solace and express ourselves to the world.

Art is also a way that we immortalize ourselves. Each human is subject to the lifespan that they are given on this planet, and when you realize that your life is going to end eventually, you start to realize that the world will move on without you. This means that you might be forgotten, at least according to our primal fear. So, we try to do things to counteract this. The most primal and animal way is to have children because then you'll live on in the world through the people who you have created to carry out their own goals and happiness in the world.

Art is a way that you can do an analysis on yourself to deeper levels. Remember the Rorschach test, a way of analyzing people where we look at blobs of ink of paper and say whatever comes to mind first? Well, all art is sort of like that, as a creator and as a viewer. As a creator, when you are creating the art, you are creating the ink blob. Sometimes it is very clear what the artist is talking about. When you look at a Norman Rockwell painting, you understand the scene that he has created because he is putting you right there in a scenario that you can recognize and understand. Other times, the artist is putting you in a place where you can't understand because you aren't meant to. This type of art can help us to explore what it feels like to other people to experience part of that world. Abstract art is not about telling you things, but rather get you to think.

Many people say that literature is the way that you can most experience another person's' consciousness, out of all of the art forms. Think about the best book you ever read. You were so into it that you couldn't put it down, and when you read it, you were nowhere else except in the world created by the writer. You were a citizen in his world, and there was nothing to do except to be there in the story and experience whatever was going on.

When you do this, you are experiencing a human mode called flow. Flow is when you are just in the moment, when you are only experiencing something that you are doing, like meditating, playing piano, running, driving, or something else. It is a state of focus and a state of creativity.

In order to know yourself, you have to be able to experience the extremes of life. You must have been able to understand the anger and express it. You must know when you feel angry and know what that feels like to you. You must be able to experience joy at the highest level, for this is an extremely human feat. You must be able to take deep pain and failure and also accept the beauty in life. You must be able to immerse yourself in the book and then go pay some bills that you have lying around, which is just menial work that you have to do. There are all sorts of things that you have to deal with that are big and small, and none are less important. It might seem that the small stuff is less important, and in many ways, it is, but the details are something that you can be vigilant with, and they are ways for you to let yourself really experience each part of life.

The number-one way to do this concretely every day and learn about you is journaling. You can journal every day a never write the same thing twice. Journaling doesn't have to be your homework. It can be fun, it can be creative and it can be a way to release yourself from the shackles of what binds you.

When you write about yourself, you are looking at yourself through the lens of another person, or at least not through your own. By writing about yourself, you are also able to tell your story. Let's talk about both of these aspects of writing.

When you write about yourself, you get to look at yourself through your own eyes, but in a more objective way. Or at least, that's the hope. When you open up the journal and start writing about yourself, and it is all negative stuff, then you should be able to tell yourself that you have a problem there. When you are writing about yourself, try to be as subjective as possible. When you find that you are not able to do this, it might mean that you are too much up in your head.

You see, we start to develop ideas and concepts about ourselves that may or may not be true. Even if they are true, they might not be so good to dwell on. Many people have problems with intrusive thoughts or automatic negative thoughts. If you are one of these people, just take your writing and see if you notice these thoughts in writing, and see if you can stop yourself and try to write out thoughts that are kinder and more accurate.

By talking about writing concerning ourselves in a more objective way, we can get more in touch with ourselves in terms of our real desires, goals, and ways of living. When we are in our heads, we don't get a really good idea of our perceptions vs. the world's perceptions around us. When we are all up in our heads about how we are, the world seems like a movie that we are starring in. When we write about our lives, it is a movie that you are writing. An objective perspective will let you talk about yourself as a friend rather than yourself. You can start to think of this guy or girl as a person who is closer to the world than to your own experience, and when you do that you reduce the number of feelings and thoughts that might get mixed up with the perspective. When you take out the emotions and thoughts and just go with the facts, you'll find that you can be fairer and more realistic about yourself. Some people will find that they have self-esteem issues that they need to deal with. Others will be more on the side of narcissism, and they will need to learn about how to reduce their selfishness and start to think more about others.

Telling a story is another big part of writing that is so beneficial to us. Writing a story can really give you some narrative that will let you be expressive and real about your life. Telling the story tells you how you feel about yourself. You can see yourself as a character in a play or movie. What is the character like? Is he or she an antagonist or protagonist? What are the values of the character what are their role in life, and their rod in the story? Once you start thinking of your life in theist way, you can start to be creative about solutions in life, because rather hand thinking about what you would do in the situation, you are actually just thinking about what your character could do, and this opens up many possibilities. Of course, if the character you have assigned yourself is the old, useless man who is not worth anything to anybody, then your story and life will reflect that. If you decry yourself as an old but wiry and motivated man, or something more positive, then your story will have all kinds of new possibilities. It is how we view ourselves, that we can see in the story, which helps us to modulate our story, which helps us to modulate our lives.

Of course, knowing yourself, and the pursuit of this knowledge must be done with kindness. If you set out to conquer yourself like a distant land for which you have a ruler's disdain, you will find that your campaign incurs more losses than it does gains. You must be engaging in this act in good faith, and you must be ready to be nice to yourself in the process. This is something that can be incredibly difficult for people to understand, and to do it is even more complicated.

Here are some strategies to know yourself and to use this to analyze others:

1. Decipher what you really want in the world
    Detach yourself from the expectations of others and try to get along with learning how to determine your own agency. Some of us lose control of our agency and forget to determine our own destiny. Realize that what you want and what you get is part of your control. There are many aspects of life that are out of your control, sure, but you should realize that you are in control of many parts of your experience.

2. Use Art in whichever form you relate to most to learn about yourself.
    Art is how we convey the non conveyable. It is how we make the abstract concrete, and it is how we bridge the gap between what is understanda-

ble and completely mysterious. As you develop your relationship with art in all its forms, you can unlock your intuition and build a deeper relationship with yourself.

Chapter 8

INTUITION

Intuition is an abstract concept. There is no way to study it, except to ask someone to describe their experience of intuition. Intuition is a combination of your spiritual self, your physical self, and your cognitive self, all coming together. It takes into account the feelings that you are experiencing, the thoughts, and the bodily sensations that you are experiencing, and it tells you what feels right at the moment.

Intuition is a deeply human thing that is not explained easily. It isn't anxiety, it isn't a fear, and it is not an emotion. Rather, it is a combination of emotion and thought and sensation that leads you to be able to make decisions. When you are feeling your intuition, try to follow it. Some people don't know what it feels like to be able to follow their intuition; they might not even be aware when they are getting the hint about something or somebody.

Intuition is that little feeling that this person is lying to you, or that slight drop in the gut when you realize that you've won a prize. It is your body reacting before your mind can. The body's an intelligent construction; we like to think of the mind as the source of intelligence in the west, but that's only partially the case. The body is to thank for some of our peer feelings and intuitive processes, and the body is what tells us when we are in danger, when we are being lied to, when a person needs genuine help, or when we are in love. A mind is a place that is filled with thoughts and ideas. The body is filled with actual sense data that is more trustable than thoughts.

Think about the last dream that you had. Where you aware that it was a dream? Probably not. There are some people who have reported that they are able to control their dreams, in a process called lucid dreaming. In this process, a person is able to point out to their sleep consciousness than they are experiencing a dream, and what they imagine is not actually real. When they do this, people can then direct their actions in the dream. They can start to be more in control, and they can find a way to be in awareness in their dreams.

Most people do not have this skill which is perfectly normal. To them, it seems like their dreams are completely real. When they are experiencing dreams, they are not able to distinguish from reality, and even though that content of the dream can be fantastical and unrealistic, they find themselves believing that everything in the dream is true and is actually happening.

This just shows how unreliable our minds are. If they are able to construct a whole new reality where you can fly or do other things that are completely unrealistic, then just imagine how far off you can get in your thinking in everyday life.

The body, on the other hand, is not so fallible. The body doesn't think, it just reacts. The body is a place where you cannot control what is happening, and that is where the truth comes in. The truth is in body language because the body just reacts. There is no cognitive filter process. This is why there is so much to be gained from studying nonverbal communication and body language. The body doesn't lie (unless you are a very good actor).

When you feel a certain way about a person in your intuition, just try to realize that it is valid. It may not be something that you want to act on, but you can start to realize that your bodily feelings of intuition are valid, and then you can start to do something with them. Many people grow up learning to ignore their intuition, for various reasons. One such reason is that they were encouraged not to express emotions when they were younger. Many younger people with strict parents are like this; they are shown or told when they are kids that expressing emotions makes them weak and that they should not express emotions for fear of being abandoned or criticized. This is a very damaging way to grow up, and it affects a person's ability to be able to trust their intuition. For a person like this, confidence will be the key to developing the ability to trust the intuition.

A person with low self-esteem will have trouble trusting their intuition because they have either learned or told themselves that their gut is not something to be trusted. This is not the case, because, for everyone, his or her inner feelings are valid. So, this person will have to learn confidence. Exposure therapy is good for this; the principles of exposure therapy states that when you are exposed to something that you are uncomfortable with for an extended period of time, you will start to learn how to deal with it more, and you will start to be able to withstand periods of exposure to the stimuli more because you are able to take the heat, so to speak. This means that people with confidence issues should look to put themselves in places outside of their comfort zone. To start, you can try to put yourself in a position to take small risks. If a person has social anxiety, they could try to get a job in a coffee shop or somewhere where they will have to interact with many people but on a limited level. This will get you thinking about how you can interact with people, and it will start to get you more comfortable with exposure to people daily. The more people that you interact with, the more you will start to learn that you are a cool and interesting person if you engage in good faith, and confidence will grow from there.

Confidence is what lets you do what you should do. Then that little feeling tells you should offer this person a job, or walk out of another situation, or drive a different route home; you do it because you are confident in yourself and you have seen yourself succeed over and over. This is something that will take a little time, and yours is patient and kind to yourself through this experience.

There is no way to record intuition; there is no way to quantify it. This is something in your soul. It is something that might take some soul-searching to do. This is something that some people feel come from your ancestor, and there is a sort of collective unisons that we are all participating in together. The idea of the collective unconscious is that we are all human beings and can relate to each other one human level. This means that our intuition will often match. Not always, but it is something that we can connect to with people who are in similar situations to us. This is something that lies simmering below the surface of our minds, is not so much on the surface. The intuition is a feeling, and it comes first before the thoughts. Thoughts are not so important. They might help you to understand your intuition, but your thoughts are not your intuition, they're an automatic process that is distracting you from whatever bodily experience you are having.

Here are some strategies to use intuition when you are reading people:

1. Slow down and clear your mind.

    If you have the chance to do so, take a minute and get away from whatever situation you are in. Talk yourself through whatever you just experienced. Try to describe to yourself what your intuition was telling you. There might be thoughts that are irrelevant that are cluttering your mind. Taking a minute to slow down and talking to yourself will give you a chance to tidy up your thinking process and figure out what you are intuiting.

2. Notice sensations in the body.

    This goes along with the practice of mindfulness. To learn what you are feeling in certain situations, you will need to check in physically and see what is happening in the body. You will start to learn to label emotions that match up with certain physical states.

3. Focus on yourself.

There might be other people who have differing opinions about the person or situation you are observing. Some you trust, and some you don't. Either way, it is important that you focus on what is important to you and what seems real and relevant at that moment. Don't let others trick you into thinking that your intuition is invalid. This will take strength and discipline. Sometimes, it is important to recognize that you are taking on the opinions of others rather than forming your own.

Chapter 9

KEY TRAITS AND SKILLS

Reading people requires significant practice and experience. There are a few practical techniques that you can use in order to strengthen your awareness and intuition.

Mindfulness is awareness, in the present moment, without judgment. Mindfulness is paying attention to whatever the object of the mindfulness is- this could be thoughts, it could be feelings, and it could be bodily sensations. Whatever the object of your attention is, you use that to practice focusing your mind for small periods of time, and then work up to larger amounts of time. Mindfulness ultimately refers to the integrated awareness of every experience in the world, whether it is bodily sensations alone, or if there are other aspects of the experience that pop up. These could include smells, sights, or whatever else. The ultimate goal is to get to a place where your mindfulness captures your entire expertise at any moment. This will take lots and lots of work.

The way to start a mindfulness practice is to start by paying attention to the breath. The breath has several physical qualities. It may have a sound. It may just be detectable by feeling the bodily sensations in your chest and nostrils. It may have other qualities, other textures that you can pay attention to. It is also a rhythmic phenomenon, which makes it a great way to tune in to the body.

When you start, just take a second to get comfortable and find where you want to sit for a minute. When you have found a place to sit or lie down, then you can just start paying attention to your breathing and focus your attention on the breath. Each time you inhale, try to feel it in your nostrils or belly, and when you breathe out, try to feel it then as well. When you are doing this, your thoughts will come into your consciousness. This is okay and to be expected. When you experience thoughts, just let them go away. You can acknowledge that they exist, but afterwards you can just return your attention to the breath. This becomes a cycle of getting distracted and then coming back to the breath, and this is the way that you can start to develop a practice of paying attention to the body. One exercise to try when you are starting out is to number each breath. When you breathe in, count 1. The exhale does not have to be counted. When you breathe in again, count 2. Then, you just continue as far as you want, or you can start over when you get to ten. This will give you a way to connect to each breath and make sure you are paying attention to each and every moment that you are experiencing the breath.

This practice has a profound effect on the body. As you start to pay more attention to the body, you will find that you are able to be more present in your life. See, most of us have the problem of lending too much credence and too much importance to our thoughts. Our thoughts are not voluntary, they are just something that happens to our bodies and minds, and it is something that we just need to learn to cope with as human beings. It is not something that you should judge yourself for. People start to care a lot about their thoughts. This might take the form of worry when a person is always concerned about the future for the past. This might take the form of over-analysis, where a person is not able to just enjoy things without spending too much time thinking about it. It might lead to a person not being able to connect with other people, and being too much in their head when they should be with another person.

Mindfulness practice fights against this imbalance and helps us to be more integrated individuals. It does this by helping to train you to learn to be a more in-the-body person than an in-the-head person. This will also lead to more emotional intelligence, where a person is able to tell more about their emotional experiences. The emotional experience is something that happens in the body. It is not a thought event, but rather a physical event. So, you can pay more attention to your emotional experience by paying attention to the body, and this will lead to a higher level of awareness.

You might ask how a higher level of awareness can lead to an increase in your ability to read people. Well, if you think about what it takes to read people, you will find that an awareness of self is important. It lets you know that when you feel angry with a person, you are actually angry and you can have more confidence in yourself because you are expressing the emotion that is what you want to express. You can trust your gut more when someone tells you something that might not be true. You can be more in touch with your experience with other people, and they will be able to trust you to be an authentic person. Just by being more authentic, you will be able to read people easier because it is something that draws other people out.

However, part of harnessing this depends on just being able to tap into the perception and intuition that you already have. One way to effectively tap into your intuition is mindfulness. The most key trait that will be the key to analyzing people is self-awareness. Before you can go and understand someone else, you must have a deep understanding of yourself in the world. A self-story is a good way to go when you are trying to establish self-awareness. This will involve some introspection. Ask yourself, "Who am I in the world? Where do I come from? What have been my challenges and successes?" When you start to answer this realistically and correctly, you will find levels of self-awareness that you did not think you could reach before. If your answer is something like, "well, it did my best in school, and I went to an okay school, and I got a job that is pretty good, and I'm single but pretty happy." This might be a sign that you are not at the level of self-awareness that you want to be at. Try to see if you can get yourself to answer something along the lines of "I am a thirty-year-old man with a good job who has a good time dating, and I love meeting people. I got a good education that have set me up for my future. I had an era of difficulty when my dad died, and I try to deal with that every day. But I will get better and better at this." This is an honest answer; this is a person who is very aware of what they are going through and know what to do with themselves. This answer has more confidence and self-awareness. This person feels good about himself or herself, and has built up a sense of resistance to feeling overwhelmed with praise or disgust.

Self-awareness can definitely be helped along with exercises. These exercises include reading difficult novels, writing about yourself, journaling, making music or art about oneself, going to therapy, having deep conversations with friends, meeting new people, and many other activates. Self-awareness cannot be found intentionally as it is an area that comes along with wisdom.

See, intelligence is the ability to think and your ability to learn. Information is something that is out there in the world. Data is the raw materials that we observe and see in the world and other people. These factors all come together and when a person is able to use this entire ad actually apply it to their world and know what is going to happen to other people when they do something, that is wisdom.

And wisdom is not something that comes overnight. Wisdom is something that comes with a difficult life and many dark nights. It is something that has to be earned, through tears, sweat, and mistakes. It is something that older people pick up as they go through life because they have seen so much. They have seen so much that they start to be able to understand the world as a big picture rather than trust the small narrow confines of their world.

Sometimes people get into a comfort zone, and they just want to stay in that zone. This can creep up on people, and you have to be intentional about getting out of your comfort zone. This means you cannot keep doing what you are doing. You must do something intentional to actually affect change. There are ways that you can get out of your comfort zone easily.

Another key trait or skill when you are learning to read people are to learn the basic tenets of behaviorism. This means you understand the conditioned stimuli versus the unconditioned stimuli. Conditioned stimuli, or CS, are when a person or animal is subjected to stimuli that they have learned something from. So, if a dog is presented with a whistle associated with getting a punishment, they will know that that means something and this is conditioned stimuli. If a dog is presented with a tasty piece of meat, as it inherently understands it is delicious, they will start to have an unconditioned response, which means they have a physical reaction that has not been taught to them before. The conditioned response is something that an animal is taught to do when presented with a CS. the conditioned response is what the animal is learning, such as the way to navigate a maze to get a piece of cheese.

Reading people takes something in the cognitive sphere, but it also takes seeing able to be self-aware. Being self-aware is being reasonably knowledgeable about yourself and the way you function in the world. It requires knowing yourself, being confident in yourself, and knowing how to question people.

How to talk to people are another basic skill if you want to read people in your verbal communication. If you want to read people, you should ask many questions and be an active listener. Being an active listener means you are reflecting what you hear and you let the person know that you understand while they are experiencing. It is when you are able to tell yourself what you need to do. When you are an active listener, you are able to hold your attention on a person for extended amounts of time. This is because you are asking questions and trying to read into the person's answers as you are trying to understand them better. This will let you get into their world, and most of the time, a person will let you ask questions because most people like talking about themselves. Most people will do this, but not all will. If you ask them a bunch of questions, some people will ask questions back, or they will be limited in their answers. This can be known as resistance, and when a person is resistant to a conversation, it means that they are not comfortable with talking to you for whatever reason.

Don't assume this reason is you. You might be just getting them at the wrong time of day, or you might have phrased your questing in a way that didn't quite make sense to them. There is a whole host of other possibilities. There might be all kinds of reasons why this person doesn't want to talk right now. Maybe they are just feeling inward, or whatever what you're trying to talk about to them is not something that they want to talk about.

As you engage in more and more of these interactions, you will notice what works and what don't. Test out strategies to see what works most smoothly for you and see if you can find a way to be a good active listener.

When you are a good active listener, you start to become more aware of how your presence affects others. See if you can hold a whole conversation with someone with only asking questions. This will be easier for some to do than others. When you are just asking questions, you're facilitating another person's thought process, and you are finding information from them as they tell a story.

Another part of reading people is making other people feel comfortable enough to share them with you. When a person is anxious or stressed, they do not want to share themselves with others. This becomes a problem when you are trying to read them because you can only read so much into a personal experience without them communicating about it with you. If people are comfortable, they will be more likely to share themselves with you and tell you what's going on with them. This means that you can be non-threatening and supportive and read people much easier as a byproduct.

CONCLUSION

Thank you for making it through to the end of *Reading People: Learn how to analyze people to identify unique personalities that are different from ourselves*, we hope that it was informative and able to provide you with all of the tools you need to achieve your goals in life.

The next step is to start applying this information into your daily life. Start writing and journaling, and you will notice how awareness of yourself leads to awareness of others. People are out there, telling their stories. All you have to do is listen.

And one last thing, please consider leaving a review on Amazon to share your thoughts of this book.

amazon.com/review/create-review/listing

www.ingramcontent.com/pod-product-compliance
Lightning Source LLC
Chambersburg PA
CBHW070427290526
45791CB00005B/1866